From Basics to Advanced Electronic Materials and Engineering for Students

Annika

Copyright © [2023]

Title: From Basics to Advanced Electronic Materials and Engineering for Students

Author's: Annika.

All rights reserved. No part of this publication may be reproduced, stored in a retrieval system, or transmitted in any form or by any means, electronic, mechanical, photocopying, recording, or otherwise, without the prior written permission of the publisher or author, except in the case of brief quotations embodied in critical reviews and certain other non-commercial uses permitted by copyright law.

This book was printed and published by [Publisher's: Annika] in [2023]

ISBN:

TABLE OF CONTENTS

Chapter 1: Introduction to Electronic Materials and Engineering   07

Definition and Importance of Electronic Materials

Overview of Electronic Engineering

Historical Developments in Electronic Materials and Engineering

Chapter 2: Fundamentals of Electronic Materials   13

Atomic Structure and Bonding

Conductors, Insulators, and Semiconductors

Crystal Structures and Lattice Defects

Electronic Band Structures

Chapter 3: Semiconductor Materials   22

Introduction to Semiconductors

Intrinsic and Extrinsic Semiconductors

Doping Techniques and Effects

Carrier Transport in Semiconductors

Chapter 4: Electronic Devices 30

Diodes

Bipolar Junction Transistors (BJTs)

Field-Effect Transistors (FETs)

Integrated Circuits (ICs)

Chapter 5: Optoelectronic Materials and Devices 38

Principles of Optoelectronics

Light Emitting Diodes (LEDs)

Photodetectors

Solar Cells

Chapter 6: Magnetic Materials and Devices 46

Introduction to Magnetism

Ferromagnetic Materials

Magnetic Storage Devices

Magnetic Sensors

Chapter 7: Nanomaterials and Nanotechnology 54

Basics of Nanomaterials

Synthesis and Characterization Techniques

Applications of Nanomaterials in Electronics

Chapter 8: Electronic Packaging and Reliability 60

Packaging Technologies for Electronic Devices

Thermal Management in Electronic Systems

Reliability and Failure Analysis

Chapter 9: Emerging Trends in Electronic Materials and Engineering 66

Organic Electronics

Flexible and Stretchable Electronics

Wearable Electronics

Internet of Things (IoT)

Chapter 10: Advanced Topics in Electronic Materials and Engineering 74

Quantum Computing

Spintronics

2D Materials and Devices

Artificial Intelligence and Machine Learning in Electronics

Chapter 11: Career Opportunities and Further Studies in Electronic Materials and Engineering 82

Job Roles and Industries

Higher Education Options and Research Opportunities

Professional Societies and Networks

Chapter 12: Conclusion 88

Recap of Key Concepts

Future Prospects in Electronic Materials and Engineering

Final Thoughts and Encouragement for Students

Chapter 1: Introduction to Electronic Materials and Engineering

Definition and Importance of Electronic Materials

In the vast realm of technology, electronic materials play a crucial role in shaping our modern world. From the smallest microprocessors to the largest power grids, electronic materials are the foundation of countless devices and systems that drive our society forward. In this subchapter, we will delve into the definition and importance of electronic materials, providing students in the field of Materials Science and Engineering with a comprehensive understanding of this fascinating subject.

Electronic materials can be broadly defined as substances that possess properties conducive to the flow of electric current. These materials exhibit a wide range of electrical behaviors, such as conductivity, resistance, and insulating properties, which make them invaluable in the design and development of electronic devices. From semiconductors like silicon and germanium to conductors like copper and aluminum, electronic materials come in various forms, each with its unique set of properties and applications.

The importance of electronic materials in the field of Materials Science and Engineering cannot be overstated. These materials are the building blocks of electronic devices, enabling the conversion, storage, and transmission of electrical energy. They are essential in the production of integrated circuits, transistors, solar cells, batteries, sensors, and countless other electronic components that power our daily lives. Understanding the properties, behavior, and fabrication methods of electronic materials is fundamental for students pursuing a career in this field.

Moreover, the study of electronic materials is crucial for advancing technology and driving innovation. As the demand for faster, smaller, more efficient, and environmentally sustainable electronic devices continues to grow, researchers and engineers need to explore new materials and improve existing ones. By understanding the properties and behaviors of electronic materials, students can contribute to the development of cutting-edge technologies, such as flexible electronics, wearable devices, renewable energy systems, and quantum computing.

In conclusion, electronic materials form the backbone of modern technology and are vital to the field of Materials Science and Engineering. This subchapter aims to provide students with a solid foundation in understanding the definition and importance of electronic materials. By comprehending the properties and behavior of these materials, students can contribute to the advancement of technology, drive innovation, and shape the future of electronic devices.

Overview of Electronic Engineering

Electronic engineering is a fascinating field that deals with the design, development, and application of electronic devices, circuits, and systems. In this subchapter, we will provide an overview of electronic engineering, highlighting its importance and relevance in today's technologically advanced world. This content is specifically tailored for students in the field of Materials Science and Engineering, who are interested in understanding the fundamentals of electronic engineering.

Electronic engineering plays a crucial role in shaping the modern world. It encompasses a wide range of technologies, from smartphones and computers to advanced medical devices and renewable energy systems. As a student of Materials Science and Engineering, gaining a fundamental understanding of electronic engineering is essential, as it lays the foundation for further exploration and innovation in this field.

At its core, electronic engineering focuses on the study of electronic components, circuits, and systems. It involves the application of principles from physics and mathematics to design, analyze, and troubleshoot electronic systems. Students will learn about semiconductors, which are the building blocks of modern electronics, and gain an understanding of how they function and interact within circuits.

Electronic engineering also covers topics such as digital and analog electronics, signal processing, control systems, and telecommunications. Through this subchapter, students will gain insights into the design and implementation of electronic devices, such as transistors, integrated circuits, and sensors. Additionally, they will learn about the principles of circuit analysis, including Ohm's law and

Kirchhoff's laws, which are essential for understanding the behavior of electronic circuits.

Furthermore, this subchapter will introduce students to various applications of electronic engineering in diverse fields. They will discover how electronic engineers contribute to the development of renewable energy systems, robotics, communication networks, and healthcare technologies. Understanding these applications will enable students to appreciate the wide-ranging impact of electronic engineering on society and inspire them to explore innovative solutions to real-world challenges.

In conclusion, the field of electronic engineering offers endless possibilities for students in Materials Science and Engineering. This subchapter provides an overview of the fundamental principles and applications of electronic engineering, serving as a stepping stone for further exploration in this field. By acquiring a strong foundation in electronic engineering, students will be well-equipped to pursue advancements in technology and contribute to the ever-evolving world of electronics.

Historical Developments in Electronic Materials and Engineering

Introduction:

The field of electronic materials and engineering has witnessed remarkable advancements over the years, shaping the world as we know it today. Understanding the historical developments in this field provides students of materials science and engineering with valuable insights into the evolution of electronic devices and their underlying materials. From humble beginnings to groundbreaking innovations, this subchapter explores the historical milestones that have paved the way for the modern era of electronics.

The Birth of Electronics:
The journey of electronic materials and engineering began with the discovery of electricity and the invention of basic electronic components. In the late 18th century, Alessandro Volta invented the first electric battery, while other pioneers like Michael Faraday and James Clerk Maxwell laid the foundation for electromagnetism. These early discoveries set the stage for further advancements in electronic materials.

The Advent of Semiconductors:
One of the most significant breakthroughs in electronic materials came in the mid-20th century with the development of semiconductors. Bell Labs researchers, including William Shockley, John Bardeen, and Walter Brattain, invented the transistor in 1947. This tiny device revolutionized the field, replacing bulky vacuum tubes and enabling the miniaturization of electronic devices.

Integrated Circuits and Moore's Law:
The 1960s witnessed the emergence of integrated circuits (ICs), which consolidated multiple transistors on a single chip. Jack Kilby and

Robert Noyce are credited with the invention of ICs, marking a major milestone in electronic materials and engineering. This breakthrough laid the foundation for Moore's Law, which predicted that the number of transistors on a chip would double approximately every two years, leading to the exponential growth of computational power.

Materials Innovations:
Advancements in electronic materials have been instrumental in the development of modern electronics. Silicon, due to its excellent semiconductor properties, became the material of choice for integrated circuits. Over time, other materials, such as gallium arsenide, gallium nitride, and indium phosphide, have gained prominence in specific applications, pushing the boundaries of performance and efficiency.

Nanotechnology and Beyond:
The turn of the 21st century saw the rise of nanotechnology, revolutionizing electronic materials and engineering once again. Nanomaterials, such as carbon nanotubes and graphene, have shown promising properties for future electronic devices. Additionally, advancements in organic materials, flexible electronics, and bioelectronics have opened new avenues for innovation.

Conclusion:
Understanding the historical developments in electronic materials and engineering is crucial for students of materials science and engineering. From the invention of transistors to the rise of nanotechnology, each milestone has contributed to shaping the modern world of electronics. By appreciating the progress made over the years, students can gain a deeper understanding of the challenges and opportunities that lie ahead in this ever-evolving field.

Chapter 2: Fundamentals of Electronic Materials

Atomic Structure and Bonding

In the fascinating realm of materials science and engineering, understanding the atomic structure and bonding is crucial. This subchapter aims to provide students with a comprehensive overview of these fundamental concepts, enabling them to delve deeper into the world of electronic materials and engineering.

At the heart of all matter lies the atom, the building block of the universe. We begin by exploring the structure of atoms, discovering their various components and their respective charges. Electrons, protons, and neutrons are introduced, along with their roles in determining the properties of different elements. We delve into the organization of electrons in energy levels or shells, discussing their distribution and how it relates to the periodic table.

Moving on, we explore the concept of atomic bonding, which governs the formation of materials. Students gain insights into the different types of bonding, including ionic, covalent, and metallic bonds. We discuss the sharing and transfer of electrons, resulting in the formation of compounds and molecules. Real-world examples are provided to illustrate the significance of bonding in various materials, from conductors to insulators.

Furthermore, the subchapter delves into the importance of atomic structure and bonding in determining material properties. Students learn how different bonding types influence characteristics such as electrical conductivity, thermal conductivity, and mechanical strength. We also touch upon the concept of crystal structures, explaining how atoms arrange themselves to form solids and how this arrangement affects material properties.

To reinforce understanding, interactive examples and exercises are incorporated throughout the subchapter. These allow students to apply their knowledge and develop a deeper grasp of the concepts discussed. Additionally, case studies and practical applications of atomic structure and bonding in the field of materials science and engineering are presented, inspiring students to connect theory with real-world advancements.

By the end of this subchapter, students will have a strong foundation in atomic structure and bonding, enabling them to comprehend the complexities of electronic materials and engineering. They will be equipped with the necessary knowledge to explore advanced topics and conduct further research in the field of materials science and engineering.

Whether aspiring to become materials scientists, engineers, or researchers, this subchapter serves as a stepping stone towards a successful and fulfilling career in the captivating world of electronic materials and engineering.

Conductors, Insulators, and Semiconductors

In the fascinating world of electronic materials and engineering, it is crucial to understand the fundamental properties of conductors, insulators, and semiconductors. These materials serve as the building blocks for countless electronic devices that have become an integral part of our daily lives. Whether you are a student of materials science and engineering or simply curious about the inner workings of electronic devices, this subchapter will provide you with a comprehensive overview of these essential components.

Conductors are materials that allow the free flow of electric current. They possess a large number of mobile charge carriers, typically electrons, which can easily move through the material when a voltage is applied. Metals, such as copper and aluminum, are excellent conductors due to their abundance of free electrons. This property makes them ideal for applications requiring efficient transmission of electricity, such as power cables and electrical wiring.

On the other hand, insulators are materials that inhibit the flow of electric current. They have a very low number of mobile charge carriers, which makes it difficult for electrons to move freely. Examples of insulators include rubber, glass, and plastic. Insulators are commonly used to provide electrical insulation and protection against electric shocks in various electrical and electronic devices.

Semiconductors occupy a unique position between conductors and insulators. They exhibit intermediate electrical conductivity and can be easily manipulated to control the flow of electric current. Silicon and germanium are the most widely used semiconducting materials. By introducing impurities into semiconductors, a process known as doping, their electrical properties can be modified. This ability to alter conductivity is crucial for designing electronic components such as diodes, transistors, and integrated circuits.

Understanding the behavior of these materials is crucial in designing and optimizing electronic devices. By carefully selecting the appropriate material for a particular application, engineers can ensure the best performance and efficiency. Moreover, advancements in materials science have led to the development of new materials with unique properties, such as graphene, which is a highly conductive material with immense potential in various electronic applications.

In conclusion, conductors, insulators, and semiconductors are the foundation of modern electronics. Their distinct electrical properties enable the transmission, control, and manipulation of electric current. As students of materials science and engineering, it is essential to grasp the concepts surrounding these materials to unlock the endless possibilities they offer in the field of electronic engineering.

Crystal Structures and Lattice Defects

In the field of Materials Science and Engineering, understanding the crystal structures and lattice defects is of paramount importance. Crystals are solids that possess a well-organized, repeating atomic arrangement, known as a lattice. This subchapter aims to delve into the fascinating world of crystal structures and lattice defects, providing students with the foundational knowledge necessary to comprehend the behavior and properties of various materials.

Firstly, let us explore crystal structures. Crystals can be classified into different types based on the arrangement of atoms within their lattice. These types include simple cubic, body-centered cubic, face-centered cubic, and more complex structures such as hexagonal close-packed and diamond structures. Each structure has its own unique arrangement of atoms, resulting in distinct properties and behaviors. By understanding crystal structures, students can predict material properties, such as mechanical strength, electrical conductivity, and optical behavior.

However, not all crystals possess a perfect atomic arrangement. Lattice defects, also known as crystal defects, are irregularities or deviations from the ideal crystal structure. These defects can occur during crystal growth, processing, or as a result of external factors such as temperature and pressure. Lattice defects can be categorized into point defects, line defects, and planar defects.

Point defects involve deviations from the ideal atomic arrangement at a single lattice point. This includes vacancies, where an atom is missing from its expected position, or interstitials, where an extra atom occupies an interstitial site. These defects can significantly influence material properties, affecting parameters such as electrical conductivity, thermal conductivity, and diffusion rates.

Line defects, also known as dislocations, occur when there is a misalignment or disruption in the atomic arrangement along a line or plane within the crystal lattice. Dislocations can greatly impact mechanical properties, such as strength, plasticity, and deformation behavior. Understanding dislocations is crucial in the design and development of materials with enhanced mechanical performance.

Planar defects involve irregularities that occur on a larger scale, such as grain boundaries and stacking faults. Grain boundaries are interfaces between two crystal grains with different orientations, while stacking faults result from the stacking of atoms in an irregular pattern. These defects can influence material behavior, including mechanical strength, electrical conductivity, and corrosion resistance.

By comprehending crystal structures and lattice defects, students can gain insights into the fundamental principles that govern the behavior and properties of materials. This knowledge lays the foundation for advanced research and engineering applications in various fields, including electronics, biomaterials, and energy storage. Furthermore, understanding how lattice defects affect material properties can lead to the development of novel materials with tailored functionalities and improved performance.

In conclusion, the study of crystal structures and lattice defects is an essential aspect of Materials Science and Engineering. This subchapter aims to provide students with a comprehensive understanding of these concepts, enabling them to analyze and predict material properties accurately. By exploring crystal structures and lattice defects, students can unlock the potential for innovation and advancement in the field of materials engineering.

Electronic Band Structures

In the world of materials science and engineering, the study of electronic band structures holds immense significance. This subchapter aims to provide students with a comprehensive understanding of electronic band structures and their role in the field.

Electronic band structures refer to the arrangement of energy levels in a solid material. These energy levels are classified into bands, each consisting of a range of possible electronic states. The behavior of electrons within these energy bands determines the electrical conductivity and other electronic properties of materials.

One of the fundamental concepts in electronic band structures is the distinction between valence and conduction bands. The valence band is the highest energy band that contains electrons at absolute zero temperature, while the conduction band lies just above the valence band and represents the energy levels where electrons can move freely. The energy gap between the two bands is known as the band gap and determines whether a material is a conductor, semiconductor, or insulator.

Understanding the electronic band structures of different materials is crucial for designing and developing new electronic devices. By manipulating the band gap, scientists and engineers can tailor the electrical properties of materials to suit specific applications. For instance, semiconductors have a small band gap, allowing for controlled movement of electrons, making them ideal for fabricating transistors and integrated circuits.

This subchapter will delve into the intricacies of electronic band structures, discussing the various factors that influence them. It will cover topics such as crystal structures, the role of doping, and the impact of temperature on band structures. Additionally, students will explore the concept of band diagrams, which visually represent the energy levels and band gaps in different materials.

To facilitate learning, this subchapter will include illustrative examples and case studies of real-world applications. By examining the band structures of materials used in electronic devices such as solar cells, LEDs, and computer chips, students will gain a practical understanding of how electronic band structures impact the functionality and performance of these devices.

Overall, this subchapter on electronic band structures aims to equip students with a solid foundation in this crucial aspect of materials science and engineering. By mastering the concepts and applications discussed, students will be well-prepared to contribute to advancements in electronic materials and devices, paving the way for future innovations in the field.

Chapter 3: Semiconductor Materials

Introduction to Semiconductors

Semiconductors are the foundation of modern electronics, and understanding their properties is crucial for students in the field of Materials Science and Engineering. This subchapter aims to provide an introduction to semiconductors, including their basic concepts, properties, and applications.

Semiconductors are materials that have properties between those of insulators and conductors. Unlike conductors, which allow the flow of electricity easily, and insulators, which do not allow the flow of electricity at all, semiconductors have the unique ability to control the flow of electrons. This property makes them ideal for use in various electronic devices.

One of the fundamental concepts to understand about semiconductors is the band gap. The band gap is the energy difference between the valence band (where electrons are held tightly) and the conduction band (where electrons can move freely). This gap determines whether a material is a conductor, insulator, or semiconductor. Semiconductors have a small band gap, allowing them to conduct electricity under certain conditions.

Intrinsic semiconductors are pure materials, such as silicon (Si) and germanium (Ge), which have their own electron and hole carriers. However, by introducing impurities into the crystal lattice, we can alter the conductivity of semiconductors. This process is known as doping and can lead to the creation of extrinsic semiconductors. Doping with elements like phosphorus or arsenic introduces additional electrons, creating an n-type semiconductor, while doping with elements like boron or gallium introduces holes, creating a p-type semiconductor.

The combination of p-type and n-type semiconductors forms the basis of one of the most important electronic devices, the diode. A diode allows current to flow in one direction while blocking it in the opposite direction. Understanding the behavior of diodes is crucial for building electronic circuits.

Semiconductors have revolutionized technology and are used in a wide range of applications, including transistors, integrated circuits, solar cells, and light-emitting diodes (LEDs). The ability to manipulate their properties has led to advancements in communication, computing, renewable energy, and many other fields.

In conclusion, this subchapter has provided a brief introduction to semiconductors, highlighting their properties, band gap, doping, and applications. As students in the field of Materials Science and Engineering, understanding semiconductors is essential for developing innovative electronic devices and technologies that shape our modern world.

Intrinsic and Extrinsic Semiconductors

Semiconductors are at the core of modern electronic devices, from computers and smartphones to solar cells and sensors. Understanding the behavior of semiconductors is crucial for students in the field of Materials Science and Engineering. In this subchapter, we will delve into the concepts of intrinsic and extrinsic semiconductors, providing a foundation for comprehending the intricate workings of these materials.

Firstly, let's explore intrinsic semiconductors. Intrinsic semiconductors are pure semiconducting materials, such as silicon or germanium, that exhibit semiconducting properties solely due to their atomic structure. These materials have a valence band, which is fully occupied by electrons, and a conduction band, which is empty at absolute zero temperature. However, at room temperature, some electrons can gain enough thermal energy to jump from the valence band to the conduction band, creating electron-hole pairs. This movement of electrons and holes allows intrinsic semiconductors to conduct electricity, albeit at a relatively low level.

Now, let's shift our focus to extrinsic semiconductors. Extrinsic semiconductors are doped with impurities to enhance their conductivity. These impurities, also known as dopants, introduce additional energy levels within the band gap of the intrinsic semiconductor. Two common types of dopants are n-type and p-type dopants. N-type dopants, such as phosphorus or arsenic, introduce extra electrons into the conduction band, increasing the conductivity of the material. On the other hand, p-type dopants, like boron or gallium, create holes in the valence band, allowing for enhanced hole conductivity.

The addition of dopants in extrinsic semiconductors alters their electrical properties significantly. This manipulation enables the design and fabrication of various electronic devices. For instance, the combination of n-type and p-type semiconductors forms a p-n junction, which is the fundamental building block of diodes, transistors, and integrated circuits.

Understanding the differences between intrinsic and extrinsic semiconductors is crucial for students in Materials Science and Engineering. It lays the foundation for comprehending more advanced topics like band diagrams, carrier transport, and device fabrication. By gaining a solid grasp of these concepts, students can contribute to the ever-evolving field of electronic materials and engineering.

In conclusion, this subchapter provided an overview of intrinsic and extrinsic semiconductors. We explored how intrinsic semiconductors conduct electricity through the movement of electron-hole pairs, as well as the introduction of dopants in extrinsic semiconductors to enhance conductivity. These fundamental concepts serve as the building blocks for further understanding the complexities of electronic materials and engineering.

Doping Techniques and Effects

In the vast field of materials science and engineering, one topic that holds immense significance is doping techniques and their effects. Doping refers to the intentional introduction of impurities into a material to alter its properties and enhance its performance. This subchapter aims to provide students in the niche of materials science and engineering with a comprehensive understanding of different doping techniques and their resulting effects.

Doping can be employed in various materials, including semiconductors, metals, and ceramics, to manipulate their electrical, optical, and mechanical properties. One of the most common doping techniques is the introduction of impurity atoms into the crystal lattice of a material. This process can be achieved through diffusion, ion implantation, or epitaxy. The choice of doping technique depends on the desired outcome and the material being doped.

The effects of doping can be profound and can significantly impact the material's performance. For instance, in semiconductors, the introduction of specific impurities can alter the material's conductivity, making it either more conductive (n-type doping) or less conductive (p-type doping). This property is essential for the design and fabrication of electronic devices such as transistors, diodes, and integrated circuits.

Moreover, doping can also modify a material's optical properties, allowing it to absorb or emit specific wavelengths of light. This property is crucial in the development of optoelectronic devices, such as lasers, LEDs, and photodetectors.

The understanding of doping techniques and their effects extends beyond electronic materials. In the field of materials science, doping is employed in various applications, including the enhancement of mechanical properties such as hardness, toughness, and wear resistance. For example, doping metals with specific elements can improve their strength and corrosion resistance, making them suitable for various engineering applications.

Additionally, this subchapter will delve into the challenges associated with doping, including the control of impurity concentration and distribution, and the potential detrimental effects of excessive doping. It will also discuss advanced doping techniques, such as molecular beam epitaxy and chemical vapor deposition, which allow precise control over the doping process.

By studying doping techniques and their effects, students in the field of materials science and engineering will gain valuable insights into the manipulation of material properties, enabling them to design and develop innovative materials for a wide range of applications.

Carrier Transport in Semiconductors

In the world of Materials Science and Engineering, semiconductors play a crucial role in the development of electronic devices that have revolutionized the way we live and communicate. Understanding the principles of carrier transport in semiconductors is fundamental for any student aspiring to delve deeper into this field. This subchapter aims to provide a comprehensive overview of carrier transport in semiconductors, shedding light on the underlying mechanisms and their significance in electronic materials and engineering.

Semiconductors are materials that possess an intermediate level of electrical conductivity, falling between conductors and insulators. This unique property arises due to the presence of energy bands in their electronic structure. In this subchapter, we will explore the behavior of charge carriers, namely electrons and holes, as they navigate through these energy bands.

One fundamental concept to grasp is the concept of charge carrier mobility. Carrier mobility refers to the ability of charge carriers to move through a semiconductor in response to an electric field. We will delve into the factors affecting carrier mobility, such as crystal structure, impurities, and temperature, and how they influence the overall conductivity of a semiconductor material.

Furthermore, we will discuss the two dominant carrier transport mechanisms in semiconductors: drift and diffusion. Drift current occurs when charge carriers move in response to an applied electric field, while diffusion current arises due to the concentration gradient of charge carriers. Understanding these mechanisms is essential to comprehend the behavior of charge carriers in various semiconductor devices, including diodes, transistors, and solar cells.

To provide a practical perspective, this subchapter will explore real-world applications and advancements in carrier transport in semiconductors. Topics such as the development of high-mobility materials, the role of carrier lifetime in photovoltaic devices, and the challenges faced in scaling down semiconductor devices will be covered.

By the end of this subchapter, students will have gained a solid foundation in the principles of carrier transport in semiconductors. They will be equipped with the knowledge to analyze and design semiconductor devices with enhanced performance, ultimately contributing to the advancement of electronic materials and engineering.

In conclusion, "Carrier Transport in Semiconductors" is a crucial subchapter that bridges the gap between the basics and advanced concepts in Materials Science and Engineering. It provides students with a comprehensive understanding of carrier transport mechanisms, their impact on semiconductor devices, and the latest developments in the field.

Chapter 4: Electronic Devices

Diodes

In the fascinating realm of electronics, diodes are fundamental components that play a crucial role in the functioning of various electronic devices. Understanding the principles and applications of diodes is essential for students venturing into the field of materials science and engineering. This subchapter explores the intriguing world of diodes, shedding light on their structure, working principles, and diverse applications.

A diode is a two-terminal electronic device that allows current to flow in only one direction, while blocking it in the opposite direction. Its structure comprises a semiconductor material, commonly made of silicon or germanium, with two regions known as the p-type and n-type. The junction between these regions forms the heart of a diode, known as the p-n junction. This junction is responsible for the diode's unique electrical behavior.

When a voltage is applied across a diode in the forward bias, the p-n junction allows current to flow easily. Electrons from the n-type region and holes from the p-type region combine at the junction, resulting in a forward current. On the other hand, when a reverse voltage is applied, the p-n junction acts as an insulator, preventing the flow of current. This behavior makes diodes ideal for rectification purposes, converting alternating current (AC) to direct current (DC).

Diodes find extensive applications in various electronic devices, making them indispensable in modern technology. They are commonly used in power supplies, where they rectify AC voltage to provide DC voltage for electronic circuits. Additionally, diodes are crucial in signal processing, as they enable the detection and demodulation of radio signals. They also serve as protection devices, preventing damage from voltage spikes and surges. Light-emitting diodes (LEDs), a specific type of diode, are widely utilized in displays, lighting, and optoelectronic applications.

As students venture further into the field of materials science and engineering, a deep understanding of diodes becomes crucial. Exploring their structure, working principles, and applications paves the way for comprehending more complex electronic devices. Additionally, diodes serve as a stepping stone for delving into advanced topics such as transistors, integrated circuits, and semiconductor physics.

In conclusion, diodes are essential components in the world of electronics. Through their unique electrical behavior, diodes enable rectification, signal processing, protection, and numerous other applications. By understanding the principles and applications of diodes, students in the field of materials science and engineering can expand their knowledge base and pave the way for further exploration into the fascinating realm of electronic materials and engineering.

Bipolar Junction Transistors (BJTs)

In the world of electronics, Bipolar Junction Transistors (BJTs) have played a significant role in amplification and switching applications. Understanding the fundamentals of BJTs is essential for students in the field of Materials Science and Engineering. This subchapter aims to introduce the basic principles behind BJTs and their applications in electronic devices.

BJTs are three-layered semiconductor devices consisting of two back-to-back p-n junctions, forming either a PNP or NPN configuration. The three layers are named the emitter, base, and collector. The BJT's functionality relies on the movement of charge carriers across the junctions, controlled by the voltage applied to the base terminal.

One of the key features that make BJTs unique is their ability to amplify weak signals. This is achieved through the process of transistor action, where a small current flowing across the base-emitter junction triggers a much larger current flow between the collector and emitter junctions. This amplification capability allows BJTs to be used in a wide range of applications, from audio amplifiers to high-frequency radio transmitters.

Students in Materials Science and Engineering will also come across the concept of BJT biasing. Biasing refers to the proper application of DC voltages to the base-emitter and base-collector junctions, ensuring the transistor operates within its desired region. This is crucial for maintaining the stability and linearity of the transistor's output.

Furthermore, the subchapter will delve into the different operating modes of BJTs, including the active mode, saturation mode, and cutoff mode. These modes dictate how the transistor behaves under different voltage and current conditions. Understanding these modes is vital for designing and analyzing BJT circuits.

In addition to amplification, BJTs are extensively used as switching devices. By manipulating the base current, BJTs can be turned on or off, allowing or blocking the flow of current through the collector-emitter junction. This property makes BJTs ideal for controlling various electronic devices, such as relays, motors, and LEDs.

Through a comprehensive exploration of BJTs, this subchapter aims to provide students in Materials Science and Engineering with a solid foundation in understanding the operation, biasing, and applications of these essential semiconductor devices. By mastering the concepts presented here, students will be equipped with the necessary knowledge to design and analyze BJT circuits while exploring advanced electronic materials and engineering concepts.

Field-Effect Transistors (FETs)

Field-effect transistors (FETs) are among the most fundamental components in modern electronic devices. In this subchapter, we will delve into the world of FETs, exploring their structure, working principles, and applications. This knowledge will be invaluable for students specializing in Materials Science and Engineering, as it forms the foundation for understanding the design and functionality of advanced electronic materials and devices.

At its core, a FET is a three-terminal device that utilizes an electric field to control the flow of current. It consists of a source, a drain, and a gate terminal. The main advantage of FETs over other types of transistors lies in their ability to offer high input impedance and low output impedance, making them ideal for many applications, including amplification and switching circuits.

One of the most common types of FETs is the Metal-Oxide-Semiconductor Field-Effect Transistor (MOSFET). MOSFETs are widely used due to their compatibility with modern integrated circuit fabrication techniques. They consist of a metal gate electrode separated from the semiconductor channel by a thin insulating layer, typically made of silicon dioxide (SiO_2). The gate terminal controls the conductivity of the channel, enabling the flow of current between the source and drain regions.

Understanding the working principle of FETs is crucial for comprehending their applications. In a MOSFET, when a positive voltage is applied to the gate terminal, an electric field is established, attracting electrons to the surface of the semiconductor channel. This creates an n-type region, allowing current to flow between the source and drain terminals. Conversely, when a negative voltage is applied, positive charges accumulate in the channel, creating a p-type region, effectively blocking the flow of current.

The versatility of FETs is evident in their applications. They are commonly used in amplifiers, allowing small input signals to control larger output signals. Moreover, FETs are vital in digital logic circuits, where they serve as switches, enabling or disabling the flow of current based on the input voltage.

In conclusion, understanding the fundamentals of Field-Effect Transistors (FETs) is essential for students specializing in Materials Science and Engineering. FETs play a crucial role in modern electronic devices and circuits, offering high input impedance and low output impedance. The Metal-Oxide-Semiconductor Field-Effect Transistor (MOSFET) is a widely used type of FET, known for its compatibility with integrated circuit fabrication techniques. By controlling the flow of current through an electric field, FETs find applications in amplifiers and digital logic circuits. Mastery of FETs will pave the way for students to explore advanced electronic materials and engineering concepts in their future studies and careers.

Integrated Circuits (ICs)

In the realm of electronics, the development of integrated circuits (ICs) has revolutionized the way we design, manufacture, and utilize electronic devices. Integrated circuits, also known as microchips or simply chips, are the building blocks of modern electronics, enabling the creation of complex systems that are smaller, faster, and more efficient than ever before. This subchapter explores the fascinating world of ICs, shedding light on their structure, fabrication processes, and applications.

At its core, an integrated circuit is a tiny electronic device that contains a multitude of interconnected components, such as transistors, resistors, capacitors, and diodes, all fabricated on a single piece of semiconductor material. These components work together to perform various functions, ranging from simple amplification to complex digital computations. The integration of multiple components onto a single chip enables the creation of highly functional electronic systems in a compact and cost-effective manner.

The fabrication process of integrated circuits involves several key steps, including wafer preparation, deposition of various thin films, lithography, etching, and metallization. These processes require precise control and expertise in materials science and engineering. The subchapter delves into each of these steps, providing a comprehensive overview of the technology behind IC manufacturing.

Furthermore, the subchapter discusses the different types of integrated circuits, such as analog, digital, and mixed-signal ICs, highlighting their unique characteristics and applications. Analog ICs are used for continuous signal processing, while digital ICs handle discrete signals, enabling the creation of complex logic circuits. Mixed-signal ICs combine both analog and digital functions to cater to a wide range of applications, including telecommunications, consumer electronics, and automotive systems.

The subchapter also explores the concept of Moore's Law, which states that the number of transistors on a chip doubles approximately every two years, leading to exponential growth in computing power. This principle has been the driving force behind the miniaturization and performance enhancement of ICs over the past few decades.

By delving into the world of integrated circuits, this subchapter aims to provide students in the field of materials science and engineering with a comprehensive understanding of this fundamental technology. From their structure and fabrication to their applications and future prospects, integrated circuits play a crucial role in shaping the modern electronic landscape. As students embark on their journey in electronic materials and engineering, a thorough understanding of ICs is essential for their success in this rapidly evolving field.

Chapter 5: Optoelectronic Materials and Devices

Principles of Optoelectronics

Optoelectronics is an exciting field that deals with the interaction of light and electronic devices. It holds immense potential for revolutionizing various industries such as telecommunications, display technology, and energy harvesting. This subchapter aims to introduce students to the fundamental principles of optoelectronics, providing them with a solid foundation to explore this rapidly evolving field.

1. Introduction to Optoelectronics: The subchapter begins with an overview of optoelectronics, highlighting its applications and significance in modern technology. Students will gain an understanding of the interdisciplinary nature of optoelectronics, combining principles from materials science, physics, and engineering.

2. Optoelectronic Devices: This section delves into the various types of optoelectronic devices, including light-emitting diodes (LEDs), photodiodes, solar cells, and lasers. Each device is explained in detail, covering their working principles, materials used, and key properties. Students will learn about the mechanisms behind light emission, absorption, and generation of electric current.

3. Semiconductor Physics: A strong foundation in semiconductor physics is crucial for understanding optoelectronic devices. This section provides an overview of band theory, electron energy levels, and the concept of doping. Students will learn how the manipulation of electronic states in semiconductors allows for the creation of optoelectronic devices.

4. **Optoelectronic Materials:** The choice of materials is critical for the performance and efficiency of optoelectronic devices. This section covers the properties and characteristics of various materials used in optoelectronics, such as III-V compounds, organic semiconductors, and quantum dots. Students will explore the advantages and limitations of different materials and their suitability for specific applications.

5. **Optoelectronic Device Fabrication:** This section focuses on the fabrication techniques employed to manufacture optoelectronic devices. Students will learn about processes like epitaxy, lithography, etching, and thin-film deposition. The importance of cleanroom environments and advanced manufacturing techniques will be emphasized.

6. **Emerging Trends and Future Directions:** To inspire students, this section highlights the latest advancements and future possibilities in optoelectronics. Topics such as nanophotonics, plasmonics, and integrated photonics will be introduced, giving students a glimpse into the cutting-edge research and technological breakthroughs that lie ahead.

By studying the principles of optoelectronics, students will gain a comprehensive understanding of this exciting field and its potential for transforming the world. This subchapter provides a solid foundation for further exploration and encourages students to actively engage in research and development in the realm of optoelectronics.

Light Emitting Diodes (LEDs)

Introduction to LEDs

In recent years, Light Emitting Diodes (LEDs) have revolutionized the field of lighting and display technology. LEDs are semiconductor devices that convert electrical energy into light. They have gained immense popularity due to their energy efficiency, long lifespan, and versatility. This subchapter will delve into the working principles, materials, and applications of LEDs, providing students with a comprehensive understanding of this groundbreaking technology.

Working Principles of LEDs

LEDs operate on the principle of electroluminescence, where light is emitted from a material when an electric current is passed through it. When a voltage is applied across the LED, electrons and holes are injected into the semiconductor material. These charge carriers recombine, releasing energy in the form of photons. The color of the emitted light depends on the energy bandgap of the semiconductor material.

Materials Used in LEDs

The choice of materials is crucial for the performance of LEDs. The most commonly used semiconductor materials for LEDs are gallium arsenide (GaAs) and gallium nitride (GaN). GaAs-based LEDs emit red and infrared light, while GaN-based LEDs emit blue and green light. By combining different materials, such as GaN with phosphorus (P) or indium (In), it is possible to create LEDs that emit a wide range of colors.

Applications of LEDs

LEDs find applications in various fields, including lighting, displays, and optoelectronics. In lighting, LEDs are replacing traditional incandescent and fluorescent bulbs due to their energy efficiency and long lifespan. LED displays are used in televisions, computer monitors, and smartphones, offering vibrant colors and high contrast ratios. Additionally, LEDs are widely used in optical communication systems, traffic lights, automotive lighting, and medical devices.

Advancements in LED Technology

The field of LED technology is constantly evolving, leading to significant advancements. Researchers are continuously striving to improve the efficiency and color quality of LEDs. This has led to the development of Organic Light Emitting Diodes (OLEDs) and Quantum Dot LEDs (QLEDs), which offer enhanced color accuracy and energy efficiency. Moreover, efforts are underway to integrate LEDs into flexible and transparent materials, opening up new possibilities for wearable electronics and smart devices.

Conclusion

LEDs have emerged as a game-changing technology in the field of lighting and displays. Their energy efficiency, long lifespan, and versatility make them a preferred choice for various applications. As students of Materials Science and Engineering, understanding the working principles and materials used in LEDs is crucial. This knowledge will enable them to contribute to the ongoing advancements in LED technology and explore new applications for this remarkable semiconductor device.

Photodetectors

Photodetectors are essential devices in the field of materials science and engineering, enabling the detection and measurement of light in various applications. They are widely used in fields such as telecommunications, imaging, environmental monitoring, medical diagnostics, and astronomy, among others. This subchapter aims to provide students with a comprehensive understanding of the principles, types, and applications of photodetectors.

In its simplest form, a photodetector converts light energy into an electrical signal. This conversion is achieved through the interaction of photons with the material used in the device. The fundamental principle behind photodetection is the generation and separation of electron-hole pairs within the material upon absorption of photons. These charge carriers can then be collected and measured, providing information about the incident light.

Various materials are used in photodetectors, each possessing unique properties that make them suitable for specific applications. Some common materials include silicon, germanium, gallium arsenide, and indium gallium arsenide. These materials can be tailored to exhibit desirable characteristics such as high sensitivity, fast response times, and low noise levels.

Photodetectors can be classified into several types based on their working principles. These include p-n junction photodiodes, avalanche photodiodes (APDs), phototransistors, and photomultiplier tubes (PMTs). Each type has its own advantages and limitations, making them suitable for different applications. For instance, APDs are often used in low-light situations due to their ability to amplify weak signals, while PMTs are employed in high-sensitivity applications that require excellent signal-to-noise ratios.

The applications of photodetectors are vast and ever-expanding. In telecommunications, photodetectors are used to convert optical signals into electrical signals for transmission and processing. In imaging, they enable the capture of high-resolution images in digital cameras and medical imaging devices. Environmental monitoring applications include detecting pollutants and measuring radiation levels. Additionally, photodetectors play a crucial role in scientific research, such as studying celestial objects in astronomy and analyzing biological samples in medical diagnostics.

Understanding the principles and applications of photodetectors is vital for students in the field of materials science and engineering. As technology continues to advance, the demand for efficient and reliable photodetection devices will only increase. By delving into the fascinating world of photodetectors, students can contribute to the development of cutting-edge technologies and make significant contributions to various industries.

Solar Cells

Introduction to Solar Cells

Solar cells, also known as photovoltaic cells, are devices that convert sunlight directly into electricity. They are an essential component of solar panels and play a crucial role in harnessing solar energy for various applications. As students in the field of Materials Science and Engineering, it is imperative to understand the working principles, materials, and engineering aspects of solar cells.

Working Principles of Solar Cells

Solar cells operate on the principle of the photovoltaic effect, which involves the conversion of light energy into electrical energy. The basic structure of a solar cell consists of two layers: an n-type semiconductor (electron-rich) and a p-type semiconductor (hole-rich). When sunlight strikes the solar cell, photons with sufficient energy excite electrons in the n-type layer, creating electron-hole pairs. These charge carriers are then separated at the junction between the two layers, generating a potential difference that drives the flow of current.

Materials for Solar Cells

Various materials have been investigated for solar cell applications, each with its own advantages and limitations. Silicon, in both crystalline and amorphous forms, is the most widely used material due to its abundance and favorable electrical properties. Other materials like gallium arsenide and cadmium telluride have higher conversion efficiencies but are more expensive or less abundant. Emerging materials like perovskites and organic polymers show great promise for achieving higher efficiencies and lower costs.

Engineering Considerations

The engineering aspects of solar cells involve optimizing their efficiency, durability, and cost-effectiveness. Several factors, such as the design of the cell, surface texturing, anti-reflection coatings, and encapsulation materials, contribute to improving the overall performance. Moreover, integrating solar cells into larger systems, such as solar panels and grids, requires careful consideration of electrical connections, voltage outputs, and system maintenance.

Applications and Future Perspectives

Solar cells find applications in various fields, ranging from residential and commercial power generation to portable electronic devices and even space exploration. As the world seeks sustainable and renewable energy sources, solar cells have gained significant attention. Ongoing research focuses on enhancing their efficiency, exploring new materials, and developing advanced manufacturing techniques to reduce costs.

Conclusion

Solar cells are at the forefront of the renewable energy revolution, and understanding their fundamental principles, materials, and engineering aspects is crucial for students in the field of Materials Science and Engineering. By harnessing the power of sunlight, solar cells provide a clean and sustainable source of electricity, making significant contributions to mitigating climate change and reducing dependence on fossil fuels. As future engineers, it is our responsibility to further advance solar cell technology to meet the world's growing energy demands while ensuring a greener and more sustainable future.

Chapter 6: Magnetic Materials and Devices

Introduction to Magnetism

Magnetism is a fascinating phenomenon that has intrigued scientists for centuries. From the discovery of lodestone in ancient Greece to the development of advanced magnetic materials used in today's technological advancements, magnetism has paved the way for numerous inventions and innovations. In this subchapter, we will delve into the fundamentals of magnetism, its various properties, and its crucial role in materials science and engineering.

At its core, magnetism is the force exerted by magnets on certain materials, such as iron, nickel, and cobalt. It is a result of the alignment of microscopic magnetic domains within these materials. These domains consist of countless tiny atomic magnets, known as magnetic moments, which align in a specific pattern to create a magnetic field.

One of the key properties of magnets is their ability to attract or repel other magnets or magnetic materials. This phenomenon is known as magnetic polarity. Like poles repel each other, whereas opposite poles attract. This property is central to the functioning of magnetic devices, such as electric motors, generators, and magnetic resonance imaging (MRI) machines.

Understanding magnetism is crucial for students in the field of Materials Science and Engineering. Magnetic materials play a vital role in a wide range of applications, including data storage, energy generation, and transportation. By studying the behavior of magnetic materials, researchers can develop new materials with enhanced magnetic properties, leading to improved technologies.

In this subchapter, we will explore the different types of magnets, including permanent magnets, electromagnets, and superconducting magnets. We will also discuss the concept of magnetic fields and how they can be visualized using magnetic field lines. Additionally, we will delve into the principles of magnetic induction and the relationship between electric currents and magnetic fields.

Furthermore, we will touch upon the magnetic properties of materials, such as ferromagnetic, paramagnetic, and diamagnetic behavior. Understanding these properties is essential for designing and engineering materials with specific magnetic characteristics.

In conclusion, magnetism is a captivating field of study that has immense significance in the realm of Materials Science and Engineering. By comprehending the principles of magnetism, students can unlock the potential for developing innovative materials and technologies. In the upcoming sections, we will delve deeper into the intricacies of magnetism, equipping you with the knowledge needed to explore the world of electronic materials and engineering.

Ferromagnetic Materials

Introduction:

In the world of Materials Science and Engineering, understanding the behavior and properties of different materials is crucial for the development of advanced technologies. One such fascinating class of materials is ferromagnetic materials. These materials exhibit a strong response to magnetic fields and have played a significant role in various applications, ranging from data storage to electrical transformers. In this subchapter, we will delve into the world of ferromagnetic materials, exploring their characteristics, applications, and underlying mechanisms.

Properties of Ferromagnetic Materials:

Ferromagnetic materials possess a unique property called ferromagnetism, which is the ability to retain a permanent magnetization even after the external magnetic field is removed. This property arises due to the alignment of magnetic moments within the material. The most commonly known ferromagnetic material is iron, but other elements like nickel and cobalt also exhibit this behavior. Understanding the properties of ferromagnetic materials is crucial for designing magnetic devices and understanding magnetic phenomena in everyday life.

Applications:

Ferromagnetic materials find extensive applications in various fields. In electrical engineering, they are used in generators, transformers, and motors due to their ability to generate and manipulate magnetic fields. In the field of data storage, ferromagnetic materials play a pivotal role in hard drives, where information is stored as magnetized regions on a rotating disk. Additionally, ferromagnetic materials are also used in medical applications, such as magnetic resonance imaging (MRI), where they enable visualization of internal body structures.

Underlying Mechanisms:

To understand the behavior of ferromagnetic materials, it is essential to comprehend the underlying mechanisms. The alignment of magnetic moments in ferromagnetic materials is a result of exchange interactions between neighboring atoms. These interactions cause the magnetic moments to align parallel to each other, leading to the formation of magnetic domains within the material. Applying an external magnetic field helps in aligning these domains, resulting in the overall magnetization of the material.

Conclusion:

Ferromagnetic materials play a crucial role in our daily lives, from electricity generation to data storage. Understanding the properties and behavior of these materials is of utmost importance for students in the field of Materials Science and Engineering. By studying the underlying mechanisms of ferromagnetism, students can contribute to the development of advanced magnetic devices and explore new applications for these materials. As we delve deeper into the world of electronic materials, ferromagnetic materials stand as a fascinating and vital area of study.

Magnetic Storage Devices

In today's digital age, where vast amounts of information are constantly being created and accessed, the need for reliable and efficient storage devices is more critical than ever. One such class of storage devices that has revolutionized the way we store and retrieve data is magnetic storage devices. These devices, based on the principles of magnetism, have played a pivotal role in the development of modern computing systems. In this subchapter, we will delve into the fascinating world of magnetic storage devices, exploring their working principles, design considerations, and future prospects.

Magnetic storage devices rely on the ability of certain materials to retain a magnetic state. The most common example of such materials is ferromagnetic materials, which possess a high magnetic permeability and can be magnetized to produce a magnetic field. The fundamental unit of a magnetic storage device is the bit, which represents a binary digit, either 0 or 1. By manipulating the magnetic state of individual bits, we can encode and store information.

One of the most iconic magnetic storage devices is the hard disk drive (HDD). HDDs consist of rotating disks coated with a thin layer of ferromagnetic material. Data is stored in concentric tracks on these disks, with each track divided into sectors. The read/write head, which hovers just above the surface of the disk, magnetizes and senses the magnetic field of the material to read and write data. HDDs offer high capacities and relatively low costs, making them suitable for various applications.

Another popular magnetic storage device is the magnetic tape. Magnetic tapes consist of a long strip of plastic coated with a thin layer of ferromagnetic material. Data is stored as a sequence of magnetized regions along the tape. Magnetic tapes are commonly used for archival and backup purposes due to their low cost, high capacity, and long-term data retention capabilities.

While magnetic storage devices have served us well for decades, advancements in technology have led to the emergence of solid-state storage devices, such as solid-state drives (SSDs). SSDs, based on flash memory technology, offer faster access times, lower power consumption, and greater durability compared to their magnetic counterparts. Nevertheless, magnetic storage devices still hold their ground due to their affordability and high capacities.

In conclusion, magnetic storage devices have played a vital role in the evolution of data storage technology. Understanding the principles behind these devices is crucial for students in the field of Materials Science and Engineering. As we continue to push the boundaries of data storage, it is essential to explore new materials and engineering techniques that can enhance the performance and capabilities of magnetic storage devices, ensuring the continued progress of computing systems in the years to come.

Magnetic Sensors

Magnetic sensors are key components in various fields of science and engineering, including materials science and engineering. These sensors play a crucial role in detecting and measuring magnetic fields, allowing for the development of innovative technologies and applications. In this subchapter, we will explore the fundamentals of magnetic sensors and their significance in electronic materials and engineering.

Firstly, it is essential to understand the basics of magnetism. Magnetic fields are created by the movement of electric charges, such as electrons. These fields have both magnitude and direction and can be characterized by properties like flux density and magnetic flux. By utilizing magnetic sensors, we can effectively measure and analyze these magnetic fields.

There are several types of magnetic sensors, each with its unique working principle and applications. One commonly used type is the Hall effect sensor. Hall sensors are based on the Hall effect, which refers to the generation of a voltage difference across a conductor when a magnetic field is applied perpendicular to the current flow. These sensors are widely employed in position sensing, current measurement, and speed detection applications.

Another type of magnetic sensor is the magnetoresistive sensor. These sensors rely on the magneto-resistive effect, where the resistance of a material changes when subjected to a magnetic field. Magnetoresistive sensors are highly sensitive and are utilized in various applications, such as magnetic field mapping, rotational speed sensing, and non-destructive testing.

Furthermore, fluxgate magnetometers are another popular type of magnetic sensor. These sensors operate based on the principle of electromagnetic induction. They consist of a ferromagnetic core surrounded by two coils, which are excited by an alternating current. The presence of a magnetic field causes changes in the core's permeability, resulting in variations in the induced voltage. Fluxgate magnetometers are widely used in geophysics, navigation systems, and scientific research.

In conclusion, magnetic sensors are fundamental tools in the field of materials science and engineering. They enable the detection and measurement of magnetic fields, allowing for the development of innovative technologies and applications. By understanding the principles and functionalities of magnetic sensors, students in this field can explore new possibilities and contribute to advancements in electronic materials and engineering.

Chapter 7: Nanomaterials and Nanotechnology

Basics of Nanomaterials

In the ever-evolving field of Materials Science and Engineering, the study of nanomaterials is gaining tremendous importance. Nanomaterials, as the name suggests, are materials with unique properties and behaviors at the nanoscale level. This subchapter will provide an introduction to the basics of nanomaterials, explaining their characteristics, synthesis methods, and potential applications.

To understand nanomaterials, it is essential to comprehend the nanoscale. At this scale, matter exhibits distinct properties due to quantum effects and surface area dominance. Nanomaterials can be classified into nanoparticles, nanowires, nanotubes, and thin films, among others, depending on their size and structure. These materials possess remarkable properties such as high strength, enhanced electrical conductivity, improved thermal stability, and unique optical properties.

The synthesis of nanomaterials involves various techniques, each tailored to produce specific structures and properties. Some common synthesis methods include chemical vapor deposition, sol-gel synthesis, and electrodeposition. These techniques allow researchers to manipulate the size, shape, and composition of nanomaterials, thus tailoring their properties for specific applications.

The importance of nanomaterials in various fields cannot be overstated. In electronics, nanomaterials are revolutionizing the development of smaller, faster, and more efficient devices. They are also widely used in energy storage and conversion systems, aiding the development of advanced batteries and solar cells. Nanomaterials find applications in medicine, where they are used in targeted drug delivery, diagnostics, and imaging. Furthermore, nanomaterials have proven to be excellent catalysts, enabling more sustainable and efficient chemical reactions.

Despite their promising potential, working with nanomaterials requires careful consideration of their unique properties and possible risks. Their small size and high surface area can lead to increased reactivity, toxicity, and environmental concerns. Therefore, it is crucial to handle nanomaterials with caution and follow appropriate safety protocols.

In summary, the basics of nanomaterials encompass their distinct properties at the nanoscale, synthesis methods, and potential applications. Nanomaterials have the potential to revolutionize various fields, from electronics to energy and medicine. However, their utilization requires a comprehensive understanding of their unique characteristics and careful handling to ensure safety. As Materials Science and Engineering students, delving into the realm of nanomaterials opens up a world of exciting research opportunities and possibilities for innovative technological advancements.

Synthesis and Characterization Techniques

In the fascinating world of Materials Science and Engineering, the ability to synthesize and characterize materials is of paramount importance. The synthesis of materials involves the creation and development of novel substances with desired properties, while characterization techniques allow scientists to analyze and understand the structure, composition, and behavior of these materials. This subchapter will delve into the various synthesis and characterization techniques used in the field, providing students with a comprehensive overview of these crucial processes.

Synthesis Techniques: Synthesis techniques are employed to fabricate materials with specific properties for various applications. Students will explore a range of synthesis methods, including chemical vapor deposition (CVD), sol-gel synthesis, physical vapor deposition (PVD), and electrochemical deposition. Each technique will be explained in detail, highlighting their principles, advantages, and limitations. Real-world examples and case studies will illustrate how these techniques have been applied to develop cutting-edge materials in different industries.

Characterization Techniques: Once materials are synthesized, it becomes essential to evaluate their properties and behavior. This section will introduce students to a plethora of characterization techniques commonly employed in Materials Science and Engineering. Students will learn about techniques such as X-ray diffraction (XRD), scanning electron microscopy (SEM), transmission electron microscopy (TEM), atomic force microscopy (AFM), and spectroscopy methods including UV-Vis, FTIR, and Raman spectroscopy. The importance of each technique in elucidating various material properties, such as crystal structure, morphology, elemental composition, and optical behavior, will be highlighted.

Hands-on Approach: To provide students with a holistic learning experience, this subchapter will encourage hands-on learning by incorporating practical examples and laboratory exercises. Students will have the opportunity to engage in simulations and experiments related to synthesis and characterization techniques. This will enable them to gain practical insights into the challenges and intricacies of the materials synthesis process, as well as the interpretation of characterization data.

Importance in Materials Science and Engineering: The subchapter will emphasize the significance of synthesis and characterization techniques in Materials Science and Engineering. Students will be exposed to the impact of these techniques on various fields, including electronics, energy, biomedical sciences, and nanotechnology. They will gain an understanding of how the synthesis and characterization of materials have revolutionized industries and contributed to technological advancements.

By the end of this subchapter, students will have a comprehensive understanding of the synthesis and characterization techniques employed in Materials Science and Engineering. They will be equipped with the knowledge to select appropriate techniques for specific material requirements and confidently interpret characterization data.

Applications of Nanomaterials in Electronics

Nanomaterials have revolutionized the field of electronics, offering unprecedented possibilities for improving the performance and functionality of electronic devices. In this subchapter, we will explore the various applications of nanomaterials in electronics, highlighting their significance in the field of materials science and engineering.

One of the most remarkable applications of nanomaterials is in the development of nanoelectronics. Nanoscale materials, such as carbon nanotubes and graphene, have shown immense potential in creating ultra-compact and high-performance electronic devices. These materials possess exceptional electrical, thermal, and mechanical properties, making them ideal for applications in transistors, sensors, and energy storage devices.

Nanomaterials also play a crucial role in enhancing the efficiency and durability of electronic displays. Quantum dots, which are semiconductor nanocrystals, have revolutionized the field of display technology. Their unique optical properties enable the production of vibrant and energy-efficient displays with a wide color gamut. Moreover, nanomaterials like graphene oxide and silver nanowires have been employed as transparent conductive films, replacing traditional indium tin oxide (ITO) in touchscreens and flexible displays.

Furthermore, nanomaterials are instrumental in the development of energy harvesting and storage devices. For instance, nanowires and nanotubes have been utilized as electrodes in lithium-ion batteries, significantly improving their charge-discharge rates and energy density. Nanomaterials, such as perovskite-based solar cells, have also emerged as a promising alternative to traditional silicon-based solar cells due to their low cost and high efficiency.

In the field of sensors and actuators, nanomaterials have opened up new possibilities for miniaturization and improved performance. Nanosensors can detect and measure various physical and chemical parameters with high sensitivity and selectivity. Carbon nanotubes and nanowires have been used as sensing elements in gas sensors, biosensors, and environmental monitoring devices. Similarly, nanomaterial-based actuators offer precise control and responsiveness for applications in robotics, microfluidics, and biomedical devices.

In conclusion, the applications of nanomaterials in electronics are vast and transformative. Their unique properties and versatility have led to advancements in nanoelectronics, displays, energy devices, sensors, and actuators. As students in the field of materials science and engineering, understanding the potential of nanomaterials in electronics is crucial for driving future innovations and pushing the boundaries of electronic devices.

Chapter 8: Electronic Packaging and Reliability

Packaging Technologies for Electronic Devices

In the rapidly evolving field of electronics, the importance of packaging technologies cannot be overstated. Electronic devices, ranging from smartphones to advanced medical equipment, require efficient packaging solutions that not only protect the sensitive components but also ensure optimal performance. This subchapter delves into the world of packaging technologies for electronic devices, providing students in the field of Materials Science and Engineering with a comprehensive understanding of this crucial aspect of electronic materials and engineering.

The subchapter begins with an introduction to the significance of packaging technologies in the electronics industry. It highlights the challenges faced by engineers in terms of miniaturization, thermal management, and signal integrity, which necessitate the development of innovative packaging techniques. Moreover, it emphasizes the role of packaging in enhancing the reliability and longevity of electronic devices.

Next, the subchapter explores various packaging techniques employed in the industry. Students will gain insights into the traditional methods such as dual in-line packages (DIP) and quad flat packages (QFP), as well as the emerging technologies such as surface mount technology (SMT) and chip-scale packaging (CSP). The advantages and limitations of each technique are discussed, allowing students to understand the trade-offs involved in selecting the most suitable packaging solution for different applications.

Furthermore, the subchapter delves into the materials used in electronic device packaging. It provides an overview of the properties and characteristics of commonly utilized materials, including ceramics, polymers, and metals. Special attention is given to the thermal and electrical properties of these materials, as they play a critical role in dissipating heat and maintaining signal integrity within the device.

To provide a comprehensive understanding, the subchapter also covers advanced packaging technologies such as 3D packaging, wafer-level packaging, and system-in-package (SiP). It explores their benefits, challenges, and potential applications in cutting-edge electronic devices.

Throughout the subchapter, real-world case studies are presented to illustrate the practical applications of different packaging technologies. These case studies highlight the role of packaging in ensuring the reliability and performance of electronic devices in diverse industries, including aerospace, automotive, and healthcare.

In conclusion, the subchapter on packaging technologies for electronic devices equips students in the field of Materials Science and Engineering with the necessary knowledge and understanding of this crucial aspect of electronic materials and engineering. By delving into the various packaging techniques, materials, and advanced technologies, students will be prepared to tackle the challenges of the ever-evolving electronics industry and contribute to the development of innovative packaging solutions.

Thermal Management in Electronic Systems

In the fast-paced world of electronics, the demand for smaller, more powerful devices is ever-increasing. However, this constant push for miniaturization and enhanced performance comes with a significant challenge – heat generation. As electronic components become more densely packed, heat dissipation becomes a critical concern. This subchapter explores the importance of thermal management in electronic systems, providing students in the field of Materials Science and Engineering with a comprehensive understanding of the principles and techniques involved.

Thermal management refers to the process of controlling and dissipating heat generated by electronic devices. Excessive heat can lead to accelerated wear and tear, reduced performance, and even catastrophic failure. Therefore, it is crucial to design electronic systems with proper cooling mechanisms to ensure optimal performance and longevity.

The subchapter begins by elucidating the fundamentals of heat transfer, introducing students to key concepts such as conduction, convection, and radiation. Understanding these principles is essential for engineers to effectively design and implement thermal management solutions. The chapter further explores the thermal properties of various materials commonly used in electronic systems, such as metals, ceramics, and polymers, as well as their impact on heat dissipation.

Next, the subchapter delves into different cooling techniques employed in electronic systems. It covers both passive and active cooling methods, discussing the advantages and limitations of each. Passive cooling techniques include heat sinks, heat pipes, and phase-change materials, while active cooling methods encompass fans, liquid cooling systems, and thermoelectric coolers. Students will gain insights into the selection and application of these cooling techniques based on the specific requirements and constraints of different electronic systems.

Furthermore, the subchapter highlights emerging trends and advancements in thermal management. It explores innovative materials and techniques, such as carbon nanotubes, graphene, and microfluidics, which show promising potential for enhanced heat dissipation in future electronic systems.

Throughout the subchapter, practical examples, case studies, and real-world applications are incorporated to help students grasp the practical implications of thermal management in electronic systems. Additionally, key challenges in thermal management, such as thermal interface resistance and hot spot cooling, are addressed, providing students with a holistic understanding of the subject.

By the end of this subchapter, students will have gained a solid foundation in thermal management principles, enabling them to design efficient and reliable cooling solutions for electronic systems. They will be equipped with the knowledge and skills necessary to tackle the evolving challenges of thermal management in the ever-advancing world of electronics.

Reliability and Failure Analysis

In the field of Materials Science and Engineering, understanding the reliability and failure analysis of electronic materials is of paramount importance. This subchapter aims to provide students with a comprehensive overview of these crucial aspects, shedding light on the factors that influence reliability and the techniques used to analyze failures.

Reliability refers to the ability of electronic materials to perform their intended functions under specified conditions for a desired period. It is a critical characteristic that determines the durability, stability, and efficiency of electronic devices. Students must grasp the fundamental concepts and mechanisms behind reliability to design and manufacture materials that can withstand the test of time.

One of the key factors influencing reliability is material degradation. Over time, electronic materials may experience various forms of wear and tear, such as mechanical stress, thermal cycling, and environmental exposure. Understanding the mechanisms of degradation and their effects on the performance of materials is vital for devising strategies to enhance reliability.

Failure analysis complements reliability by investigating the causes and effects of material failures. It involves identifying the root causes of failures and developing methods to prevent future occurrences. Failure analysis techniques include visual inspection, non-destructive testing, and material characterization, among others. By analyzing failed materials, students can gain valuable insights into the weaknesses and limitations of different electronic materials and develop strategies to mitigate potential failures.

Furthermore, failure analysis plays a crucial role in quality control and assurance. By identifying and rectifying failures during the manufacturing process, students can ensure that electronic materials meet the required standards for reliability, minimizing the likelihood of product recalls and customer dissatisfaction.

Throughout this subchapter, students will explore real-life case studies and examples that highlight the importance of reliability and failure analysis. They will learn about the different types of failures encountered in electronic materials and the techniques employed to identify and mitigate them. Additionally, students will gain insights into the latest advancements in reliability testing and failure analysis, equipping them with the knowledge and skills necessary to excel in the field.

In conclusion, reliability and failure analysis are vital components of Materials Science and Engineering. By understanding the factors influencing reliability and employing effective failure analysis techniques, students can design and manufacture electronic materials that are robust, durable, and efficient. This subchapter aims to empower students with the knowledge and skills required to contribute to the advancement of electronic materials and ensure their reliability in various applications.

Chapter 9: Emerging Trends in Electronic Materials and Engineering

Organic Electronics

In recent years, the field of organic electronics has emerged as a promising area of research and development in the realm of Materials Science and Engineering. This subchapter aims to introduce students to the fundamental concepts and advancements in organic electronics, providing a comprehensive understanding of this exciting field.

Organic electronics refers to the use of organic materials, primarily carbon-based polymers, as the building blocks for electronic devices. These materials possess unique properties that make them highly suitable for various applications, ranging from flexible displays and solar cells to sensors and transistors. The advantages of organic electronics lie in their lightweight, low-cost production, and compatibility with flexible substrates, enabling the creation of novel devices with enhanced functionality.

One of the key components of organic electronics is organic semiconductors. These materials exhibit semiconducting behavior, allowing for the controlled flow of electrical charges. Students will gain insights into the structural and electrical properties of organic semiconductors, including their energy levels, charge transport mechanisms, and the influence of molecular structure on device performance.

The design and fabrication of organic electronic devices will also be explored. Students will learn about the methods used to deposit and pattern organic thin films, as well as the various techniques employed for device characterization. By understanding the principles behind device fabrication, students will be equipped with the knowledge to optimize the performance of organic electronic devices and address challenges such as stability and efficiency.

Furthermore, this subchapter will delve into the diverse applications of organic electronics. Students will discover how organic materials have revolutionized the field of displays, enabling the development of flexible, lightweight, and even transparent screens. The use of organic solar cells as an alternative energy source will also be explored, highlighting their potential for clean and sustainable power generation.

To provide a holistic understanding, the subchapter will touch upon the future prospects and emerging trends in the field of organic electronics. Students will be introduced to cutting-edge research areas such as organic bioelectronics and stretchable electronics, which demonstrate the limitless possibilities of organic materials in various interdisciplinary fields.

By the end of this subchapter, students will have a solid foundation in organic electronics, enabling them to understand, analyze, and contribute to the advancements in this ever-evolving field. This knowledge will empower students to explore innovative solutions and contribute to the future of electronic materials and engineering.

Flexible and Stretchable Electronics

In recent years, the field of electronics has witnessed a remarkable transformation with the emergence of flexible and stretchable electronics. These revolutionary technologies have opened up new possibilities for the development of next-generation electronic devices that can conform to various shapes and withstand mechanical deformations. This subchapter explores the fascinating world of flexible and stretchable electronics, providing students in the field of Materials Science and Engineering with a comprehensive understanding of this cutting-edge area.

Flexible electronics refer to electronic circuits and devices that can be bent, twisted, folded, and even stretched without compromising their functionality. This is made possible through the use of flexible substrates, such as plastic or thin metal foils, which replace the rigid materials traditionally employed in conventional electronics. The flexibility of these substrates enables the creation of thin, lightweight, and conformable electronic devices that can be integrated into a wide range of applications, including wearable electronics, flexible displays, and biomedical devices.

Stretchable electronics take flexibility a step further by allowing electronic materials and devices to stretch and deform like rubber. This unique property is achieved by incorporating stretchable materials, such as elastomers or nanomaterials with tunable mechanical properties, into the electronic components. Stretchable electronics have emerged as a promising technology for applications that require conformability to irregular surfaces, such as electronic skins, smart textiles, and bio-integrated sensors.

The subchapter delves into the materials and fabrication techniques employed in flexible and stretchable electronics. Students will explore the properties and design considerations of flexible substrates, stretchable materials, conductive polymers, and nanomaterials, providing them with a comprehensive foundation to develop their own flexible and stretchable devices. Furthermore, the subchapter introduces students to the characterization methods and challenges associated with evaluating the mechanical and electrical properties of these unique materials.

Additionally, the subchapter discusses the current state-of-the-art in flexible and stretchable electronic devices, showcasing various examples and applications. Students will gain insights into the operation principles of flexible displays, wearable sensors, and stretchable energy storage devices, among others. Furthermore, the potential future directions and challenges in the field will be addressed, fostering critical thinking and encouraging students to explore and contribute to this exciting field.

Overall, this subchapter on flexible and stretchable electronics aims to equip students in the field of Materials Science and Engineering with the knowledge and understanding required to delve into this rapidly evolving area. By exploring the materials, fabrication techniques, and applications of flexible and stretchable electronics, students will be prepared to contribute to the development of innovative electronic devices that can transform industries and enhance our daily lives.

Wearable Electronics

In recent years, the field of wearable electronics has gained tremendous popularity, revolutionizing the way we interact with technology. From smartwatches and fitness trackers to augmented reality glasses and smart clothing, wearable electronics have become an integral part of our daily lives. This subchapter will provide an overview of wearable electronics, exploring the materials and engineering principles behind their development, with a focus on the interests of students in the field of Materials Science and Engineering.

Section 1: Introduction to Wearable Electronics

This section will introduce the concept of wearable electronics and its significance in today's society. It will discuss the various applications and benefits of wearable devices, such as health monitoring, activity tracking, communication, and fashion.

Section 2: Materials for Wearable Electronics

Here, we delve into the materials used in wearable electronics, covering topics such as flexible and stretchable materials, conductive textiles, and biocompatible materials. The section will explore their properties, fabrication techniques, and the challenges associated with integrating these materials into wearable devices.

Section 3: Power and Energy Harvesting

One key aspect of wearable electronics is their power source. This section will discuss different energy harvesting techniques, including solar cells, thermoelectric generators, and piezoelectric materials. Students will learn how these techniques can be utilized to power wearable devices efficiently.

Section 4: Sensing and Actuation

Sensors play a crucial role in wearable electronics, enabling devices to gather data and respond to the user's needs. This section will explore various sensor types commonly used in wearables, such as accelerometers, heart rate monitors, and temperature sensors. Additionally, it will cover actuation techniques, including haptic feedback and shape-memory alloys.

Section 5: Challenges and Future Trends

In this final section, we address the challenges faced by wearable electronics, including durability, comfort, and privacy concerns. Students will also be introduced to future trends and emerging technologies in the field, such as bio-integrated electronics and electronic tattoos.

Conclusion:

Wearable electronics offer immense potential in enhancing our lives and transforming various industries. This subchapter has provided an overview of the materials, engineering principles, and applications of wearable electronics, catering specifically to the interests of students in the field of Materials Science and Engineering. By understanding the fundamentals of wearable electronics, students can contribute to the development of innovative, user-friendly, and sustainable wearable devices, shaping the future of technology.

Internet of Things (IoT)

In today's digital age, the Internet of Things (IoT) has emerged as a revolutionary concept that is shaping the future of technology. It has become an integral part of our lives, connecting devices and enabling them to communicate and share data with each other. From smart homes to wearable devices, IoT has the potential to transform various industries and improve our quality of life.

The Internet of Things refers to the interconnection of everyday objects, such as appliances, vehicles, and even buildings, through the internet. These objects are embedded with sensors, software, and other technologies that enable them to collect and exchange data. This data can then be analyzed and used to enhance efficiency, productivity, and decision-making processes.

As students studying Materials Science and Engineering, understanding the principles and applications of IoT is crucial. The integration of materials and electronic engineering plays a vital role in the development of IoT devices. From the creation of sensors and actuators to the design of energy-efficient systems, materials science and engineering contribute significantly to the success of IoT.

One of the key challenges in IoT is the design and development of materials that are compatible with these interconnected devices. Materials must possess properties such as flexibility, durability, and low power consumption to ensure seamless integration within the IoT ecosystem. Advancements in nanotechnology have paved the way for the creation of smart materials, which can sense changes in their environment and adapt accordingly.

Furthermore, the security and privacy of IoT devices are paramount. Students must understand the potential risks associated with IoT and learn techniques to mitigate these risks. The interconnected nature of IoT devices makes them vulnerable to cyber-attacks and unauthorized access. Therefore, the development of secure materials and encryption techniques is essential to protect sensitive data and maintain user privacy.

In conclusion, the Internet of Things is revolutionizing the way we interact with technology. As students in the field of Materials Science and Engineering, it is important to grasp the fundamental concepts of IoT and its applications. By combining knowledge of materials and electronic engineering, we can contribute to the development of innovative and sustainable IoT devices that will shape the future of technology.

Chapter 10: Advanced Topics in Electronic Materials and Engineering

Quantum Computing

In recent years, the field of quantum computing has emerged as a groundbreaking area of research, revolutionizing the world of information processing. This subchapter will introduce students to the fascinating world of quantum computing, providing a comprehensive overview of its principles, applications, and potential impact on the field of materials science and engineering.

Quantum computing is a branch of computer science that leverages the principles of quantum mechanics to perform computations. Unlike classical computers that rely on binary digits or bits (0s and 1s) to store and process information, quantum computers utilize quantum bits or qubits. These qubits can exist in multiple states simultaneously, thanks to a phenomenon known as superposition. This unique property of qubits allows quantum computers to perform parallel computations, exponentially increasing their computational power compared to classical computers.

One of the key applications of quantum computing that holds great promise for the field of materials science and engineering is the ability to simulate and optimize complex molecular systems. Quantum computers can efficiently model the behavior of atoms and molecules, helping scientists design new materials with enhanced properties. This capability can revolutionize the development of new materials, such as more efficient batteries, advanced semiconductors, and stronger yet lightweight materials for aerospace applications.

Furthermore, quantum computing has the potential to revolutionize cryptography and secure communication. Quantum computers can solve certain complex mathematical problems much faster than classical computers, posing a potential threat to conventional cryptographic systems. As a result, researchers are actively working on developing quantum-resistant encryption algorithms to ensure secure communication in the age of quantum computing.

While quantum computing is still in its infancy, students studying materials science and engineering can benefit greatly from understanding its principles and potential applications. As the technology matures, the demand for professionals with expertise in quantum computing will undoubtedly increase. By gaining a solid foundation in quantum computing, students can position themselves at the forefront of this exciting field, opening up new opportunities for research, innovation, and career advancement.

In conclusion, quantum computing has the potential to revolutionize the field of materials science and engineering. Its unique computational power and ability to simulate molecular systems can lead to the development of new materials with enhanced properties. Additionally, the field of cryptography will require quantum-resistant encryption algorithms to ensure secure communication in the future. By delving into the principles and applications of quantum computing, students can equip themselves with the necessary knowledge and skills to thrive in this transformative field.

Spintronics

Spintronics, short for spin-based electronics, is a rapidly evolving field that holds immense potential for revolutionizing the way we design and develop electronic devices. In this subchapter, we will delve into the fascinating world of spintronics, exploring its fundamental concepts, applications, and future prospects.

At its core, spintronics aims to harness the intrinsic property of electrons called "spin." Unlike conventional electronics that rely on the charge of electrons, spintronics exploits the spin orientation of electrons to store, process, and transmit information. By manipulating the spin of electrons, researchers can create novel devices with enhanced functionality and improved performance.

One of the key components in spintronics is the spin valve, a device that utilizes the phenomenon of giant magnetoresistance (GMR). GMR refers to the significant change in electrical resistance when a magnetic field is applied. This technology has paved the way for the development of high-density, non-volatile memory devices, such as magnetic random-access memory (MRAM). MRAM offers fast read/write times, low power consumption, and high endurance, making it a promising alternative to conventional memory technologies.

Another exciting area within spintronics is the field of spintronic sensors. These sensors exploit the spin-dependent transport properties of materials to detect and measure various physical quantities, such as magnetic fields, temperature, and strain. Spintronic sensors have found applications in diverse fields, including automotive, aerospace, and biomedical industries, due to their high sensitivity, robustness, and miniaturization potential.

Furthermore, spintronics has opened up new possibilities for quantum computing and quantum information processing. Quantum bits, or qubits, which are the fundamental units of information in quantum systems, can be encoded in the spin states of electrons. By manipulating and controlling the spin of electrons, researchers aim to achieve quantum entanglement and superposition, enabling exponentially faster computation and secure communication.

As materials scientists and engineers, understanding the properties and behaviors of spintronic materials is crucial. Materials like magnetic metals, semiconductors, and insulators play a vital role in spintronics devices. Exploring the synthesis, characterization, and design of these materials is essential in pushing the boundaries of spintronics technology.

In conclusion, spintronics offers a promising avenue for advancing the field of electronics. Its unique ability to utilize the spin of electrons opens up possibilities for developing faster, more efficient, and multifunctional devices. As students in materials science and engineering, diving into the realm of spintronics will provide you with a solid foundation in this cutting-edge field, allowing you to contribute to the ongoing advancements and innovations in electronic materials and engineering.

2D Materials and Devices

In recent years, the field of Materials Science and Engineering has witnessed a revolution with the discovery and exploration of 2D materials. These materials, consisting of a single layer of atoms or molecules, hold tremendous promise for the development of next-generation electronic devices. This subchapter will delve into the fascinating world of 2D materials and their applications in electronic engineering.

2D materials, such as graphene, boron nitride, and transition metal dichalcogenides (TMDs), possess unique properties that make them highly suitable for electronic applications. For instance, graphene, which is a single layer of carbon atoms arranged in a hexagonal lattice, exhibits exceptional electrical conductivity and mechanical strength. This makes it an ideal candidate for electronic devices, including transistors, sensors, and flexible displays.

Furthermore, TMDs like molybdenum disulfide (MoS_2) and tungsten diselenide (WSe_2) offer a wide range of electronic properties, from conducting to insulating, depending on their thickness and structure. These materials have been utilized in the development of optoelectronic devices, solar cells, and energy storage systems.

One of the key advantages of 2D materials is their atomically thin nature, which enables unprecedented control over their electrical, optical, and mechanical properties. Researchers can manipulate these materials at the atomic level, tailoring their characteristics to meet specific device requirements. This level of precision opens up new possibilities for designing and fabricating electronic components with enhanced performance and functionality.

Furthermore, the integration of 2D materials with traditional semiconductors has led to the development of novel hybrid structures. These structures combine the unique properties of 2D materials with the well-established fabrication processes of the semiconductor industry. Such hybrids have been employed in high-performance transistors, photodetectors, and memory devices, paving the way for advanced electronic technologies.

As students of Materials Science and Engineering, understanding the fundamental properties and potential applications of 2D materials is crucial for staying at the forefront of this rapidly evolving field. By exploring the synthesis techniques, characterization methods, and device architectures associated with 2D materials, you will be well-equipped to contribute to the development of cutting-edge electronic technologies.

In conclusion, the emergence of 2D materials has revolutionized the field of electronic engineering. Their exceptional properties, atomically thin structure, and ability to be integrated with traditional semiconductor materials make them highly attractive for next-generation devices. By studying and harnessing the potential of these materials, students like you can play a significant role in shaping the future of electronic materials and engineering.

Artificial Intelligence and Machine Learning in Electronics

In recent years, the fields of Artificial Intelligence (AI) and Machine Learning (ML) have made remarkable strides, revolutionizing various industries, and the electronics sector is no exception. This subchapter explores the significant impact of AI and ML in electronics and its applications, specifically within the domain of Materials Science and Engineering.

AI and ML are technologies that enable machines to learn from data and make intelligent decisions without explicit programming. In the context of electronics, these technologies have paved the way for significant advancements, enhancing the performance, efficiency, and functionality of electronic devices.

One key application of AI and ML in electronics is in the design and optimization of electronic materials. By analyzing vast amounts of data, AI algorithms can identify patterns, correlations, and properties of different materials, leading to the discovery of new materials with desirable properties. This has accelerated the development of advanced semiconductors, superconductors, and other electronic components, resulting in faster and more efficient devices.

Moreover, AI and ML techniques are employed in the manufacturing processes of electronic devices. By utilizing real-time data monitoring and advanced analytics, these technologies can optimize production parameters, minimize defects, and improve yield rates. This not only reduces manufacturing costs but also ensures the production of high-quality electronic materials and components.

In addition to material design and manufacturing, AI and ML have also revolutionized the field of electronics through intelligent systems and devices. For instance, AI-powered sensors are capable of collecting and analyzing data from the environment, enabling smart systems to adapt and respond to changing conditions. This has led to the development of autonomous vehicles, smart homes, and wearable electronics, enhancing our daily lives and increasing efficiency.

As students in the field of Materials Science and Engineering, understanding the role of AI and ML in electronics is crucial. These technologies are driving innovation, and their integration with electronic materials is reshaping the industry. By familiarizing themselves with AI and ML concepts, students can actively contribute to the advancement of electronic materials and engineer intelligent electronic systems.

In conclusion, AI and ML have brought significant advancements to the field of electronics, particularly within Materials Science and Engineering. From material design and manufacturing optimization to the development of intelligent systems, these technologies have transformed the industry. As students, embracing AI and ML will enable you to be at the forefront of this exciting revolution, shaping the future of electronics.

Chapter 11: Career Opportunities and Further Studies in Electronic Materials and Engineering

Job Roles and Industries

In the ever-evolving field of materials science and engineering, there is a wide range of job roles and industries that students can explore. This subchapter aims to provide an overview of the diverse career opportunities available to students pursuing a degree in materials science and engineering.

One of the most common job roles in this field is that of a materials engineer. These professionals are responsible for developing, testing, and evaluating materials used in various industries such as aerospace, automotive, electronics, and healthcare. They work closely with scientists, technicians, and other engineers to ensure that the materials meet the specific requirements of a particular application. Materials engineers may specialize in areas such as metals, polymers, ceramics, or composites, depending on their interests and expertise.

Another exciting job role within the materials science and engineering field is that of a research scientist. These individuals conduct fundamental research to discover and develop new materials with enhanced properties or novel applications. Research scientists often work in academic institutions, government laboratories, or private research organizations. Their work is vital in pushing the boundaries of knowledge and driving innovation in industries such as energy, electronics, and medicine.

Apart from traditional engineering roles, materials science and engineering graduates can also pursue careers in quality control and assurance. These professionals play a crucial role in ensuring that the materials produced meet the required standards and specifications. They may work in manufacturing facilities, conducting rigorous testing and analysis to verify the quality and performance of materials.

In recent years, there has been a growing demand for materials engineers in the renewable energy sector. With the increasing focus on sustainable energy sources, materials engineers are involved in developing advanced materials for solar panels, wind turbines, and energy storage devices. This area offers exciting opportunities for students interested in contributing to a greener and more sustainable future.

Moreover, the field of biomedical materials has gained significant attention in recent years. Biomedical engineers and materials scientists work together to develop materials that are compatible with the human body, such as biocompatible implants, tissue scaffolds, and drug delivery systems. This interdisciplinary field offers a unique opportunity to combine knowledge from materials science, engineering, and biology to improve healthcare outcomes.

Overall, the field of materials science and engineering offers a wide range of job roles and industries for students to explore. Whether it is working as a materials engineer, research scientist, quality assurance professional, or in specialized fields like renewable energy or biomedical materials, students can find rewarding careers that contribute to technological advancements and societal well-being.

Higher Education Options and Research Opportunities

As students pursuing a career in Materials Science and Engineering, it is crucial to explore the various higher education options available to you. In this subchapter, we will discuss the different paths you can take to further your knowledge and skills in this field, as well as the exciting research opportunities that await you.

One of the primary options for higher education is pursuing a Bachelor's degree in Materials Science and Engineering. This undergraduate program provides a solid foundation in the fundamentals of the discipline. It covers topics such as crystallography, material characterization, mechanical behavior, and electronic properties. Additionally, it offers hands-on laboratory experience, allowing you to apply theoretical concepts to real-world scenarios. A Bachelor's degree equips you with the necessary expertise to work in various industries or pursue advanced degrees.

For those seeking more specialized knowledge, a Master's degree in Materials Science and Engineering is an excellent option. This program delves deeper into specific areas of interest, such as biomaterials, nanomaterials, or electronic materials. It also offers opportunities for research projects and collaborations with industry professionals. A Master's degree opens doors to advanced positions in research and development, consulting, or academia.

If you aspire to become a leading expert in the field, a Doctorate in Materials Science and Engineering is the pinnacle of higher education. This program focuses on conducting groundbreaking research and making significant contributions to the field. As a doctoral student, you will have the chance to work closely with renowned professors and experts, pushing the boundaries of knowledge in materials science. A Ph.D. not only qualifies you for prestigious positions in academia but also opens doors to leadership roles in research and development.

In addition to higher education options, exploring research opportunities is essential for students in Materials Science and Engineering. Research allows you to investigate new materials, develop innovative technologies, and contribute to scientific advancements. Many universities and institutions offer undergraduate research programs, allowing you to gain valuable hands-on experience while working alongside experienced researchers. These research opportunities provide a platform to apply classroom knowledge to real-world problems, fostering critical thinking and problem-solving skills.

Graduate students can also engage in cutting-edge research projects. By working closely with professors and industry partners, you can contribute to the development of new materials, explore novel fabrication techniques, or investigate emerging fields such as renewable energy or biotechnology. Research not only enhances your technical skills but also allows you to contribute to the advancement of society and make a lasting impact.

In conclusion, higher education options and research opportunities are abundant for students in Materials Science and Engineering. Whether you choose to pursue a Bachelor's, Master's, or Doctorate degree, each path offers unique benefits and opens doors to exciting career prospects. Engaging in research further enhances your knowledge and skills, allowing you to contribute to the cutting-edge developments in the field. Embrace these opportunities and embark on a journey towards becoming a skilled materials scientist or engineer.

Professional Societies and Networks

In the ever-evolving field of Materials Science and Engineering, it is crucial for students to stay connected and up-to-date with the latest advancements, research, and opportunities. One way to achieve this is by actively participating in professional societies and networks. These platforms provide a wealth of resources, knowledge sharing, and networking opportunities that can greatly enhance your academic and professional journey.

Professional societies and networks are organizations that bring together individuals who share a common interest in a specific field. For students in Materials Science and Engineering, various societies exist worldwide, such as the Materials Research Society (MRS), American Ceramic Society (ACerS), and Institute of Electrical and Electronics Engineers (IEEE). These societies offer a wide range of benefits, including access to journals, conferences, workshops, webinars, and career development resources.

By joining a professional society, students gain exposure to cutting-edge research through publications and conferences. Journals published by these organizations are valuable sources of new discoveries and innovative techniques, keeping students informed about the latest trends in the field. Attending conferences and workshops organized by these societies provides opportunities to interact with renowned researchers, industry professionals, and fellow students. These interactions offer a chance to network, collaborate, and gain insights into potential career paths.

Additionally, professional societies often offer scholarships, grants, and awards specifically tailored to students. These opportunities can help fund research projects, attend conferences, or pursue further education. Such recognition can enhance a student's resume and open doors to prestigious institutions or companies.

Networking is a vital component of professional growth, and joining a professional society provides an excellent platform to build connections. Engaging with professionals in the field can lead to internships, job opportunities, and mentorship. Many societies have online platforms or forums where members can discuss research, seek advice, and share resources. This collaborative environment fosters learning and development, making it easier for students to navigate the complexities of the field.

In conclusion, professional societies and networks are invaluable resources for students in Materials Science and Engineering. By actively participating in these organizations, students gain access to a plethora of research, networking, and career development opportunities. It is highly recommended that students take advantage of these platforms to enhance their academic journey and prepare for a successful career in this exciting field.

Chapter 12: Conclusion

Recap of Key Concepts

In this subchapter, we will take a moment to recap some of the key concepts we have covered so far in our journey from basics to advanced electronic materials and engineering. As students in the field of materials science and engineering, it is crucial to have a solid understanding of these fundamental concepts, as they form the building blocks of our knowledge and skills.

First and foremost, we explored the fundamentals of electronic materials, including their classification, properties, and applications. We learned about the different types of materials used in electronics, such as conductors, semiconductors, and insulators, and how their unique properties make them suitable for specific electronic devices.

Next, we delved into the world of semiconductors, which play a central role in modern electronics. We explored the concept of energy bands and bandgaps, which determine the electrical conductivity of semiconductors. We also learned about doping, a process that introduces impurities into semiconductors to alter their electrical properties and create p-n junctions, the basis of diodes and transistors.

Furthermore, we discussed the principles and applications of various electronic devices, including diodes, transistors, and integrated circuits. We examined the characteristics and operation of these devices, as well as their importance in the design and fabrication of electronic systems. We also touched upon the advancements in nanotechnology and its impact on electronic materials and devices.

Additionally, we explored the concept of materials engineering, which involves the design, development, and optimization of materials for specific applications. We discussed various techniques used in materials engineering, such as crystal growth, thin film deposition, and lithography. We also highlighted the importance of materials characterization techniques, including microscopy, spectroscopy, and electrical measurements, in understanding the properties and behavior of electronic materials.

Finally, we emphasized the significance of interdisciplinary collaboration in the field of electronic materials and engineering. We highlighted the need for collaboration between materials scientists, electrical engineers, and other experts to develop innovative electronic devices and systems.

In conclusion, this subchapter served as a recap of the key concepts we have covered throughout our journey from basics to advanced electronic materials and engineering. As students in the field of materials science and engineering, it is essential to have a strong grasp of these concepts to excel in our studies and future careers. By understanding the fundamentals of electronic materials and engineering, we are equipped to contribute to the exciting advancements and innovations in this rapidly evolving field.

Future Prospects in Electronic Materials and Engineering

As students of Materials Science and Engineering, you are embarking on a journey that holds immense potential for the future. The field of electronic materials and engineering is rapidly evolving and promises exciting advancements that will shape the world we live in. In this subchapter, we will explore the future prospects in electronic materials and engineering and shed light on the opportunities that lie ahead.

One of the most significant areas of growth in electronic materials and engineering is in the field of nanotechnology. As technology continues to miniaturize, the need for materials that can operate at nanoscale becomes crucial. Nanomaterials, such as carbon nanotubes and graphene, are revolutionizing the electronics industry. These materials possess remarkable electrical, thermal, and mechanical properties, making them ideal for use in high-performance devices. The future holds immense potential for further research and development in this field, leading to even more efficient and powerful electronic devices.

Another promising avenue in electronic materials and engineering is the development of flexible electronics. Traditional rigid electronics are being replaced by flexible and stretchable versions that can conform to any shape. These flexible electronics enable the creation of wearable devices, smart textiles, and even implantable medical devices. As the demand for wearable technology continues to rise, there will be ample opportunities for students in this field to contribute to the development of innovative and user-friendly electronic materials.

Furthermore, the future of electronic materials and engineering lies in sustainable and eco-friendly solutions. With increasing concerns about the environmental impact of electronic waste, researchers are exploring materials that are biodegradable and recyclable. The development of sustainable electronic materials not only reduces the carbon footprint but also opens up new possibilities for the industry. Students in this field can play a vital role in finding solutions to minimize waste and promote a greener future.

Lastly, the integration of electronic materials with other disciplines, such as biomedical engineering and renewable energy, presents exciting prospects for students. The fusion of electronics with medicine has paved the way for wearable health monitoring devices and implantable sensors. Similarly, the incorporation of electronic materials in renewable energy technologies, such as solar cells and energy storage devices, holds the key to a sustainable future. By combining knowledge from various fields, students can contribute to the development of interdisciplinary solutions that address some of the world's most pressing challenges.

In conclusion, the future prospects in electronic materials and engineering are promising and diverse. From nanotechnology to flexible electronics, sustainable solutions to interdisciplinary applications, the opportunities for students in this field are vast. By staying informed about the latest advancements and actively participating in research and development, you can be at the forefront of shaping the future of electronic materials and engineering. So, embrace the possibilities, expand your horizons, and embark on a journey that will undoubtedly leave a lasting impact on the world.

Final Thoughts and Encouragement for Students

As we conclude this book, "From Basics to Advanced: Electronic Materials and Engineering for Students," we want to express our admiration for your dedication and commitment to the field of Materials Science and Engineering. Throughout these pages, we have delved into the fundamental concepts that form the backbone of this discipline, and we hope that this journey has been both enlightening and inspiring for you.

Materials Science and Engineering is a vast and ever-evolving field that plays a crucial role in shaping the world we live in. From the development of advanced electronic devices to the creation of innovative materials with unique properties, your work as students in this domain is of utmost importance. You have chosen a path that not only demands intellectual rigor but also offers immense opportunities to make a significant impact on society.

As you embark on your journey as materials scientists and engineers, we encourage you to embrace curiosity and a thirst for knowledge. Never stop asking questions, challenge the status quo, and seek innovative solutions to the problems you encounter. The field of Materials Science and Engineering thrives on innovation, and it is the creativity and ingenuity of individuals like you that push the boundaries of what is possible.

Remember that setbacks and failures are an inevitable part of any scientific endeavor. Don't be discouraged by these obstacles but rather see them as stepping stones towards growth and improvement. Learn from your mistakes, adapt your approach, and persevere. Some of the most groundbreaking discoveries in history were born out of perseverance and the refusal to give up.

Furthermore, we want to emphasize the importance of collaboration and interdisciplinary thinking. Materials Science and Engineering often require expertise from various fields, such as chemistry, physics, and electrical engineering. By collaborating with others and leveraging their knowledge, you can create synergistic solutions that are greater than the sum of their parts.

Finally, always keep in mind the potential impact of your work. Whether you are developing new materials for renewable energy, improving the efficiency of electronic devices, or finding novel ways to recycle and reduce waste, your contributions can have far-reaching effects on society and the environment. Your passion for Materials Science and Engineering can be a driving force for positive change.

In conclusion, we hope that this book has equipped you with a solid foundation in Electronic Materials and Engineering. As you continue your journey, remember to stay curious, embrace challenges, collaborate, and always strive for excellence. The future of Materials Science and Engineering lies in your hands, and we have no doubt that you will shape it in remarkable ways. Best of luck on your path ahead!

www.ingramcontent.com/pod-product-compliance
Lightning Source LLC
LaVergne TN
LVHW010556070526
838199LV00063BA/4989